Yum, Yum

and

Sit, Ned!

'Yum, Yum' and 'Sit, Ned!'
An original concept by Caroline Walker
© Caroline Walker 2023

Illustrated by Gareth Robinson

Published by MAVERICK ARTS PUBLISHING LTD
Studio 11, City Business Centre, 6 Brighton Road,
Horsham, West Sussex, RH13 5BB
© Maverick Arts Publishing Limited August 2023
+44 (0)1403 256941

A CIP catalogue record for this book is available at the British Library.

ISBN 978-1-84886-980-6

www.maverickbooks.co.uk

This book is rated as: Red Band (Guided Reading)
It follows the requirements for Phase 2/3 phonics.
Most words are decodable, and any non-decodable words are familiar, supported by the context and/or represented in the artwork.

Yum, Yum and Sit, Ned!

By Caroline Walker

Illustrated by Gareth Robinson

The Letter Y

Trace the lower and upper case letter with a finger. Sound out the letter.

*Down,
around,
up,
down,
around*

*Down,
lift,
down,
down*

4

Some words to familiarise:

pancakes   hob   pan

High-frequency words:

up   no   said   put   it
all   in   the   on

Tips for Reading 'Yum, Yum'

- Practise the words listed above before reading the story.
- If the reader struggles with any of the other words, ask them to look for sounds they know in the word. Encourage them to sound out the words and help them read the words if necessary.
- After reading the story, ask the reader how Ned got a pancake.

Fun Activity

Discuss what toppings you would put on pancakes!

"But no pancakes for Ned," said Dad.

"Yes, Dad," said Tim.

"Put it all in," said Dad.

Mix, mix, mix.

"Put the hob on," said Tim.

It got hot in the pan.
Hot, hot, hot!

"Toss it up!" said Dad.

Up, up, up!

"Add the toppings," said Dad.

Yum, yum, yum!

The Letter S

Trace the lower and upper case letter with a finger. Sound out the letter.

Around, around

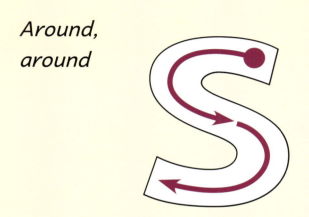

Around, around

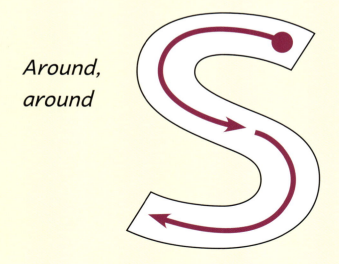

Some words to familiarise:

High-frequency words:

said go off on the
up of it was we

Tips for Reading 'Sit, Ned!'

- Practise the words listed above before reading the story.
- If the reader struggles with any of the other words, ask them to look for sounds they know in the word. Encourage them to sound out the words and help them read the words if necessary.
- After reading the story, ask the reader if Ned and Tim won.

Fun Activity

Discuss what other tricks Ned could do.

Ned sat.

"Go!" said Tim.

"Stop," said Tim.

Ned sat on the ramp.

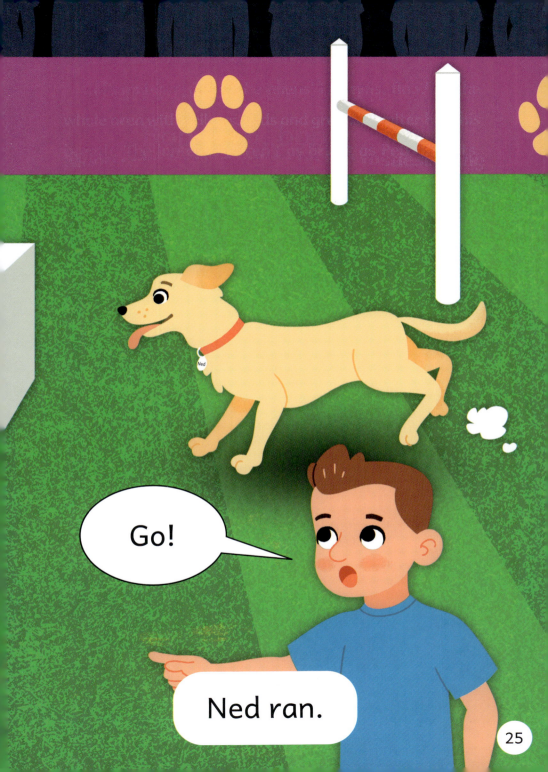

"Up!" said Tim.

Ned got up on the box.

Ned ran out of the tunnel.

He sat. It was the end.

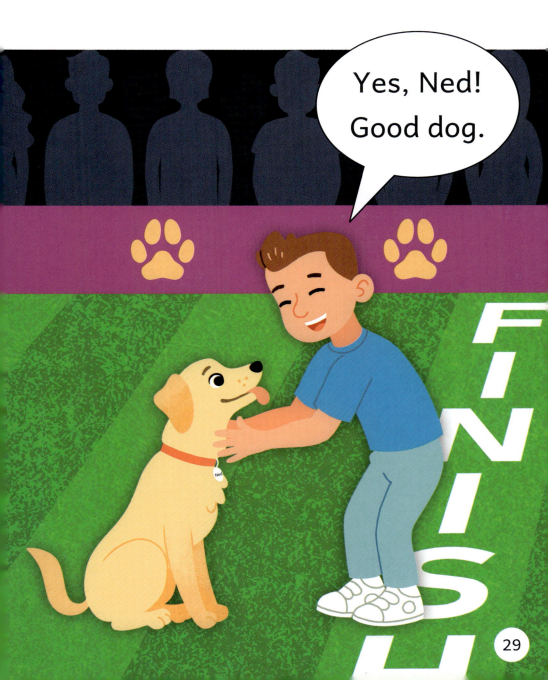

Book Bands for Guided Reading

The Institute of Education book banding system is a scale of colours that reflects the various levels of reading difficulty. The bands are assigned by taking into account the content, the language style, the layout and phonics. Word, phrase and sentence level work is also taken into consideration.

Maverick Early Readers are a bright, attractive range of books covering the pink to white bands. All of these books have been book banded for guided reading to the industry standard and edited by a leading educational consultant.

To view the whole Maverick Readers scheme, visit our website at www.maverickearlyreaders.com

Or scan the QR code above to view our scheme instantly!